Common Core Connections
Language Arts
Grade 1

Carson-Dellosa Publishing, LLC
Greensboro, North Carolina

Credits
Content Editor: Jeanette M. Ritch, M.S. Ed.
Copy Editor: Sandra Ogle

 Visit *carsondellosa.com* for correlations to Common Core, state, national, and Canadian provincial standards.

Carson-Dellosa Publishing, LLC
PO Box 35665
Greensboro, NC 27425 USA
carsondellosa.com

ISBN 978-1-62442-793-0

04-293141151

Table of Contents

Introduction

What Are the Common Core State Standards for English Language Arts?

The standards are a shared set of expectations for each grade level in the areas of reading, writing, speaking, listening, and language. They define what students should understand and be able to do. The standards are designed to be more rigorous and allow for students to justify their thinking. They reflect the knowledge that is necessary for success in college and beyond.

As described in the Common Core State Standards, students who master the standards in reading, writing, speaking, listening, and language as they advance through the grades will exhibit the following capabilities:

1. They demonstrate independence.
2. They build strong content knowledge.
3. They respond to the varying demands of audience, task, purpose, and discipline.
4. They comprehend as well as critique.
5. They value evidence.
6. They use technology and digital media strategically and capably.
7. They come to understand other perspectives and cultures.*

How to Use This Book

This book is a collection of practice pages aligned to the Common Core State Standards for English Language Arts and appropriate for first grade. Included is a skill matrix so that you can see exactly which standards are addressed on the practice pages. Also included are a skill assessment and a skill assessment analysis. Use the assessment at the beginning of the year or at any time of year you wish to assess your students' mastery of certain standards. The analysis connects each test item to a practice page or set of practice pages so that you can review skills with students who struggle in certain areas.

* © Copyright 2010. National Governors Association Center for Best Practices and Council of Chief State School Officers. All rights reserved.

© Carson-Dellosa • CD-104608

Common Core State Standards*
Alignment Matrix

Pages	12	13	14	15	16	17	18	19	20	21	22	23	24	25	26	27	28	29	30	31	32	33	34	35	36	37	38	39	40	41	42	43	44	45	46	47	48	49	50	51
1.RL.1	•	•												•	•																									
1.RL.2			•																																					
1.RL.3				•	•																																			
1.RL.4	•					•	•																																	
1.RL.5								•	•																															
1.RL.6										•																														
1.RL.7											•	•																												
1.RL.9													•																											
1.RL.10		•	•	•	•	•	•			•	•	•	•	•	•	•																								
1.RI.1																	•																							
1.RI.2																		•	•																					
1.RI.3																				•		•																		
1.RI.4																					•																			
1.RI.5																				•		•																		
1.RI.6																							•																	
1.RI.7																																								
1.RI.8																								•																
1.RI.9																										•														
1.RI.10																	•	•	•		•				•	•		•												
1.RF.1																													•											
1.RF.1a																														•										
1.RF.2																																								
1.RF.2a																																	•							
1.RF.2b																																		•	•					
1.RF.2c																																		•	•					
1.RF.2d																																			•					
1.RF.3																																					•	•		
1.RF.3a																																						•	•	•
1.RF.3b																																								
1.RF.3c																																								
1.RF.3d																																•									
1.RF.3e																																								
1.RF.3f																																								
1.RF.3g																																								
1.RF.4					•																																			
1.RF.4a																							•	•			•													
1.RF.4b																												•												
1.RF.4c																																								
1.W.1																																								
1.W.2																																								
1.W.3																																								
1.W.5																																								
1.W.6																																								
1.W.7																																								
1.W.8																																								
1.L.1																																								
1.L.1a																																								
1.L.1b																																								
1.L.1c																																								
1.L.1d																																								
1.L.1e																																								
1.L.1f																																								
1.L.1g																																								
1.L.1h																																								
1.L.1i																																								
1.L.1j																																								
1.L.2																																								
1.L.2a																																								
1.L.2b																																								
1.L.2c																																								
1.L.2d																																								
1.L.2e																																					•			
1.L.4		•																																						
1.L.4a																					•																				
1.L.4b																																								
1.L.4c																																								
1.L.5																																								
1.L.5a																																								
1.L.5b																																								
1.L.5c																																								
1.L.5d																																								
1.L.6																																								

Common Core State Standards* Alignment Matrix

Pages	52	53	54	55	56	57	58	59	60	61	62	63	64	65	66	67	68	69	70	71	72	73	74	75	76	77	78	79	80	81	82	83	84	85	86	87	88	89	90
1.RL.1																																							
1.RL.2																																							
1.RL.3																																							
1.RL.4																																							
1.RL.5																																							
1.RL.6																																							
1.RL.7																																							
1.RL.9																																							
1.RL.10																																							
1.RI.1																																							
1.RI.2																																							
1.RI.3																																							
1.RI.4																																							
1.RI.5																																							
1.RI.6																																							
1.RI.7																																							
1.RI.8																																							
1.RI.9																																							
1.RI.10																																							
1.RF.1																																							
1.RF.1a																																							
1.RF.2																																							
1.RF.2a																																							
1.RF.2b																																							
1.RF.2c																																							
1.RF.2d																																							
1.RF.3																																							
1.RF.3a																																							
1.RF.3b	●	●																																					
1.RF.3c			●	●																																			
1.RF.3d					●																																		
1.RF.3e						●																																	
1.RF.3f							●	●																															
1.RF.3g									●	●																													
1.RF.4											●																												
1.RF.4a																																							
1.RF.4b																																							
1.RF.4c												●																											
1.W.1													●	●																									
1.W.2															●	●	●																						
1.W.3																		●																					
1.W.5																			●	●																			
1.W.6																					●	●																	
1.W.7																							●																
1.W.8																								●															
1.L.1													●						●	●	●			●															
1.L.1a																									●														
1.L.1b																										●													
1.L.1c																									●														
1.L.1d																																		●					
1.L.1e						●	●																																
1.L.1f																											●												
1.L.1g																												●											
1.L.1h																													●										
1.L.1i																														●									
1.L.1j																															●								
1.L.2																																●							
1.L.2a																									●														
1.L.2b																																●							
1.L.2c																																	●						
1.L.2d									●	●																													
1.L.2e																																							
1.L.4												●																											
1.L.4a																																							
1.L.4b																																			●				
1.L.4c						●	●																																
1.L.5												●																											
1.L.5a																																			●	●	●		
1.L.5b																																			●	●	●		
1.L.5c																						●																	
1.L.5d																																						●	
1.L.6																																							●

Read the story. Answer the questions.

Kerry's Farm

Kerry works on a farm. She wears a straw hat when she is working. She takes care of the plants. She waters the flowers. She picks the berries. She places the flowers and berries into her basket. She brings her basket to the farm stand. The farm stand is where she sells the flowers and berries. Many people buy them. They love to smell the flowers. They try the berries. The farm is not fancy. The farm takes hard work. Kerry does not mind. The farm is her favorite place to be.

1. Where does Kerry work? _____

2. What does she place in her basket? _____

3. Where does she sell her things? _____

4. Who buys the plants? _____

5. What does Kerry wear? _____

Fire

Fire is very hot. Fire is a pretty color. Some fires are helpful. They keep campers warm at a campfire. Fire helps roast marshmallows. Fire in the grill can cook hot dogs. Fire lets you see in the dark. But, some fires can be dangerous. A fire in a fireplace is safe when a grown-up is watching it. Grown-ups know how to take care of a fire. If a fire gets big, the firefighter gets a call. The firefighter comes to **put the fire out**. The firefighter uses a big hose. The water can **put the fire out**.

6. Why is fire helpful? _____

_____

7. Why is a fire dangerous? _____

8. Who uses a big hose? _____

9. What does it mean to **put the fire out**? _____

10. Look at the words in the box. Place the words in the left or right side of the chart.

mane	plan	dim	Sal	plane	man	dime	sale

Short Vowel Words	Long Vowel Words

11. How many syllables does each word have? Place it in the correct box.

backpack	ball	elephant	fox	girl	raincoat

1	2	3

12. Read the words. Use each one in a sentence.

   A. was _____

   B. the _____

   C. once _____

   D. have _____

13. Circle the consonant digraph in each word.

    A. ship

    B. shop

    C. dish

14. Circle the consonant digraph in each word.

    A. with

    B. that

    C. think

15. Circle the consonant digraph in each word.

    A. chop

    B. chip

    C. much

16. Look at the words. Break them apart by sound.

Word	First Sound	Middle Sound	Ending Sound
hut			
lip			

17. Write a sentence about how you feel about recess. _____

_____

18. Write three sentences about how to put on a shirt.

First, _____.

Then, _____.

Finally, _____.

19. Write two sentences about a time you forgot something.

_____

_____

20. Write the alphabet below.

Uppercase Letters

Lowercase Letters

21. Write the noun and make it plural.

    A. nap _____

    B. mat _____

    C. fin _____

22. Names need capital letters. Write the names correctly.

    A. jan _____

    B. sam _____

    C. scott _____

23. Add ending punctuation to the end of each sentence.

    A. Will you go to the pond with me ____

    B. I want to go now ____

    C. We have to wait for Dad ____

24. Place commas in the sentence to separate the words.

Kris goes to the grocery store to buy milk eggs and cheese.

After you score each student's skill assessment pages, match any incorrectly answered problems to the table below. Use the corresponding practice pages for any problem areas and ensure that each student receives remediation in these areas.

Answer Key:
1. farm; 2. flowers, berries; 3. farm stand; 4. many people; 5. straw hat; 6. Answers include: It keeps us warm, it is good for cooking, and it lets us see in the dark. 7. It is very hot and it can get big. 8. firefighter; 9. stop the fire (with water); 10. short vowel words: plan, dim, Sal, man; long vowel words: mane, plane, dime, sale. 11. 1—fox, ball, girl; 2—backpack, raincoat; 3—elephant; 12. Answers vary but should have a subject, a verb, and the irregular word indicated. 13. A. sh, B. sh, C. sh; 14. A. th, B. th, C. th; 15. A. ch, B. ch, C. ch; 16. h-u-t, l-i-p; 17. Answers will vary but should have a subject and a verb. 18. Answers will vary but should indicate sequence. 19. Answers will vary. 20. A, B, C, D, E, F, G, H, I, J, K, L, M, N, O, P, Q, R, S, T, U, V, W, X Y, Z; a, b, c, d, e, f, g, h, i, j, k, l, m, n, o, p, q, r, s, t, u, v, w, x, y, z; 21. A. naps, B. mats; C. fins; 22. A. Jan, B. Sam, C. Scott; 23. A. ?, B. !, C. .; 24. Commas are placed after *milk* and after *eggs*.

Common Core State Standards*		Test Items	Practice Pages
Reading Standards for Literature			
Key Ideas and Details	1.RL.1–1.RL.3	1–4	12–16, 25–26
Craft and Structure	1.RL.4–1.RL.6	17	12, 17–21
Integration of Knowledge and Ideas	1.RL.7, 1.RL.9	5	22–24
Range of Reading and Level of Text Complexity	1.RL.10	1–5	13–18, 21–27
Reading Standards for Informational Text			
Key Ideas and Details	1.RI.1–1.RI.3	7–8	28–31, 33
Craft and Structure	1.RI.4–1.RI.6	6, 9	31, 32–34
Integration of Knowledge and Ideas	1.RI.7–1.RI.9	6, 7	35, 36, 38
Range of Reading and Level of Text Complexity	1.RI.10	6–9	28–30, 32, 36, 37, 39
Reading Standards: Foundational Skills			
Print Concepts	1.RF.1	22, 23	40, 41
Phonological Awareness	1.RF.2	10, 16	42–46
Phonics and Word Recognition	1.RF.3	10–16	42, 47–61
Fluency	1.RF.4	1–10	17, 34, 37, 38, 40, 62, 63
Writing			
Text Types and Purposes	1.W.1–1.W.3	17–19	64–69
Production and Distribution of Writing	1.W.5–1.W.6	17–19	70–73
Research to Build and Present Knowledge	1.W.7–1.W.8	18–19	74–75
Language			
Conventions of Standard English	1.L.1–1.L.2	21–24	48, 58–61, 66, 70–72, 75–84
Vocabulary Acquisition and Use	1.L.4–1.L.6	9	12, 32, 58, 59, 63, 73, 85–90

© Carson-Dellosa • CD-104608

Name_____

Read the story. Answer the questions.

At the Pond

One warm spring day, the ducklings decided to go to the pond. The ducklings wanted to go for a swim.

"Can we go too?" the chicks asked.

"Chicks cannot swim," the ducklings laughed.

"We will run in the tall grass and look for bugs. Please let us come."

So the ducklings and the chicks set off for the pond.

The ducklings swam in the pond. They splashed in the water. The chicks ran in the tall grass. They looked for bugs. The ducklings and the chicks had a lot of fun. After a while, the ducklings and the chicks were tired. They were **exhausted** from playing hard. They missed their mothers. They missed their nests. It was time to go home.

1. The main idea is the big point of the story. Which sentence tells the main idea?
   A. Ducklings have fun swimming.
   B. Chicks and ducklings hatch from eggs.
   C. Both ducklings and chicks can have fun at the pond.

2. A detail is a small point in the story. Which sentence tells a detail?
   A. They looked for bugs.
   B. Both ducklings and chicks can have fun at the pond.
   C. A flower grew by the pond.

3. What does the word **exhausted** mean?
   A. tired
   B. silly
   C. angry

☐ I can answer questions about the main idea and details of a story.
☐ I can find a new word in a story and know its meaning.

Read the story. Answer the questions.

Hide-and-Seek

"Will you play hide-and-seek?" Jake asked his mother. "I don't have time. I have to find some tape," Jake's mother said. "I'll help," Jake said. He looked high and low. He found his mother's tape in a pile on her desk.

"Will you play hide-and-seek with me?" Jake asked his brother. "I don't have time. I have to find my kite," his brother said. "I'll help," Jake said. He looked high and low. He found his brother's kite by the gate.

"Will you play hide-and-seek with me?" Jake said to his father. "I don't have time. I have to find my rope," his father said. "I'll help," Jake said. He looked high and low. He found his father's rope by the rake.

"Will you play hide-and-seek with me?" Jake asked his sister. "I don't have time. I have to find my dime," his sister said. "I'll help," Jake said. He looked high and low. He found his sister's dime behind the drapes.

"Too bad no one has time to play hide-and-seek!" Jake laughed.

1. Draw a line from each family member to the object he or she lost.

mother	rope
father	kite
sister	tape
brother	dime

2. What did Jake want to do?
   A. take a hike
   B. play hide-and-seek
   C. fly a kite

3. Where did Jake find his mother's tape?
   A. by the gate
   B. on her desk
   C. behind the drapes

☐ **I can answer questions about the main idea and details of a story.**
☐ **I can read first-grade text.**

Read the story. Answer the questions.

The Fox and His Trap

One day, Fox was busy making something. Turtle came by.

"What are you making, Fox?" Turtle asked. "Nothing," Fox answered. "It looks like a trap to me," Turtle said as he walked away.

Soon, Mouse came by. "What are you making, Fox?" Mouse asked. "Nothing," Fox answered. "It looks like a trap to me," Mouse said as he crawled away.

Before long, Duck came by. "What are you making, Fox?" Duck asked. "Nothing," Fox answered. "It looks like a trap to me," Duck said as she waddled away.

Just as Fox finished, Rabbit came by. "What did you make, Fox?" Rabbit asked. "A home for a rabbit," Fox said. "It looks like a trap to me," Rabbit said. "Nonsense," Fox said. "Come closer and have a look."

"But I don't think I will fit," Rabbit said.

"Nonsense!" Fox laughed. "It's big enough for me." Fox crawled inside. With Fox inside, Rabbit shut the latch. The door was shut tight. Rabbit hopped off, saying, "It looks like a trap to me."

1. Who got caught in Fox's trap?
   A. the turtle
   B. the mouse
   C. the fox

2. Why did Fox want to make a trap?
   A. He liked to build things.
   B. He wanted to catch Rabbit.
   C. He had extra wood.

3. Why do you think the fox always said, "Nothing," when others asked what he was making? _____

4. Why do you think Rabbit knew to shut the latch? _____

☐ I can understand key details.
☐ I can understand the message of a story.
☐ I can read first-grade text.

Read the story. Answer the questions.

A Place for Little Toad

Little Toad hopped out of the pond. "Where are you going, Little Toad?" the other toads asked. "I'm tired of living in this pond with so many toads," Little Toad said. "I need more room." So Little Toad hopped away.

Soon, he met a rabbit. "Little Toad, why are you so far from home?" the rabbit asked. "I need more room," Little Toad said. "You can live with me. A lot of room is under the roots of this old tree," the rabbit said.

"No, thank you," Little Toad said. "This is no place for me."

Next, he met a bee. When he told the bee his story, the bee buzzed, "You cannot live with me. You would get stuck in my honey." Little Toad said, "Don't worry, bee, a honey tree is no place for me." Little Toad hopped away.

Then, Little Toad met a dog. Before he could say a word, the dog barked and chased Little Toad away.

Little Toad hopped and hopped. Before he knew it, he had hopped all of the way back to his pond. The other toads were happy to see him. They moved over to make room for him. Little Toad settled in and smiled. "Now, this is the place for me!" he said.

1. Write a sentence to tell the main event of the story. _____

_____

Draw the setting. It is where the story takes place.	Draw a character from the story with Little Toad.

☐ I can describe the main event of a story.
☐ I can describe the setting and the characters of a story.
☐ I can read first-grade text.

Read the story. Answer the questions.

A Hot Summer Day

It was a hot summer day. "This is a good day to be lazy. I will lie in the shade of the apple tree," Billy said.

Soon, Katie came skipping by. "What are you doing?" she asked.

"Oh, nothing," Billy replied.

"I think I will do nothing, too," Katie said. She sat down next to Billy.

They saw an ant pulling a big leaf. A ladybug flew onto Katie's hand. A grasshopper hopped by. A bee landed on a flower. "It is fun doing nothing," Billy and Katie said.

1. Write a sentence to tell the main event of the story. _____

_____

Draw the setting. It is where the story takes place.	Draw Billy and Katie.

- ☐ I can describe the main event of a story.
- ☐ I can describe the setting and the characters of a story.
- ☐ I can read first-grade text.

Name_____

Read the poem.

Please come here so you can hear.
Can't you see the deer, my dear?

Please come to the sea to see
If a flea can really flee.

Please come to school to learn to write right
and add two plus two too.
Maybe you can come next week if you're not
still feeling weak from the flu.

Answer the questions.

1. Find a word or a group of words in the poem that shows feeling. Write it on the line. _____

2. Write a sentence about the word or the group of words you wrote. _____

_____

3. Have you ever felt this way? Write a sentence about it. _____

_____

☐ I can identify a word or a phrase (group of words) in a poem that shows feeling.
☐ I can read with fluency.
☐ I can read first-grade text.

© Carson-Dellosa • CD-104608

17

Read the poem.

I
love
spring
more than
anything.
More than anything,
I love spring.

I like to sing in the spring
about the flowers spring brings
and how I wish
I were a bird with wings.

I like to hold a kite
by its string
and fly on a swing.
I feel like a king
in the
spring.

Answer the questions.

1. Find a word or a group of words in the poem that shows feeling. Write it on

the line. _____

2. Write a sentence about the word or the group of words you wrote. _____

_____

3. Have you ever felt this way? Write a sentence about it. _____

_____

☐ I can find a word or a phrase (group of words) in a poem that shows
   feeling.
☐ I can write about a word or a phrase in a poem that shows feeling.
☐ I can read first-grade text.

Name_____

Some books tell stories. They are called fiction. Some books give facts. They are called nonfiction.

Read the titles. Check what kind of book it is.

Book Title	Story (Fiction)	Fact (Nonfiction)
1. *The Life of the President*		
2. *Natalie's Great Clubhouse in Her Yard*		
3. *How to Peddle a Bike*		
4. *The History of the State of Texas*		
5. *Mike's Field Trip to the Zoo*		

Find three books. Write down the titles. Check what kind of book it is.

Book Title	Story (Fiction)	Fact (Nonfiction)
6.		
7.		
8.		

- ☐ I can understand books that tell stories and books that tell facts.
- ☐ I can understand fiction and nonfiction books.

A **fiction** book tells a story. It may be about a character or an event. A fiction book has a plot. A plot is made up of the events that create a story.

A **nonfiction** book tells facts. It can be about anything true. A nonfiction book gives information.

Look in your library or classroom. Find books that are fiction or nonfiction. Write the titles in the lists below.

Fiction Books	Nonfiction Books

1. How can you tell a fiction book from a nonfiction book? _____

_____

2. Which type of book do you like to read? _____

☐ I can find fiction and nonfiction books.
☐ I can tell the difference between storybooks and fact books.

Name_____

Read the story. Answer the questions.

The Race

Sammy Snail was sad. He wanted to run in the big race, but he was too slow. Robby Rabbit hopped up to Sammy Snail. "Why are you so sad?" he asked.

"I am too slow to be in the big race," Sammy Snail cried.

"Sammy Snail, you are too slow!" Robby Rabbit laughed as he hopped down the road.

Kami Kangaroo saw Sammy Snail on her way to the race. "Why are you crying?" she asked.

"I am too slow to be in the big race," cried Sammy Snail.

"Don't cry. I will help you," Kami Kangaroo. said. She picked up Sammy Snail. She dropped him in her kangaroo pouch.

Soon, it was time for the big race. Robby Rabbit and Kami Kangaroo raced together. As they hopped to the finish line, Kami Kangaroo took Sammy Snail out of her pouch. She set him down across the finish line. Sammy Snail won the big race!

1. Who are the characters in this story? _____

2. Which animal told Sammy Snail he was too slow? _____

3. Which animal helped Sammy Snail? _____

4. A narrator tells a story but is not a character in the story. This story has a narrator. Write a sentence from the narrator's part of the text. _____

_____

☐ **I can tell who is telling a story at different places in a text.**
☐ **I can read first-grade text.**

Read the story. Answer the questions.

Mary's Surprise

Mary woke up early. Mom and Dad were asleep. She wanted to surprise them. Mary dressed herself. She combed her hair and went downstairs.

Mary placed some cereal in two bowls. She added some milk. She made toast with jam. Mary placed the food on a tray. She took it up the stairs to Mom and Dad. They were surprised to have breakfast in bed.

1. Color the picture. Look at the items on the tray.

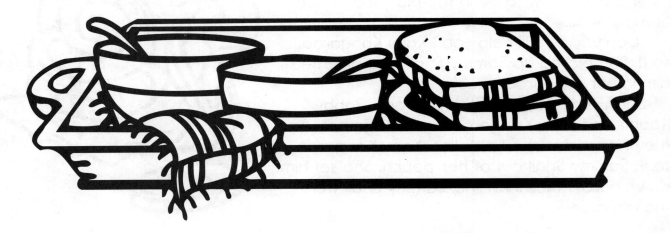

2. What items did you color? _____

3. Who are the characters? _____

4. What is the setting, or where the story takes place? _____

5. What was the main event that happened? _____

☐ **I can use pictures and details in a story to describe characters, settings, and events.**
☐ **I can read first-grade text.**

Name_____

Read the story. Answer the questions.

The Show

Ruby and her friends put on a music show. The show was in July. Judy played a tune on her flute. Hugo played the bugle. Luke marched in his new uniform. Susan danced in her cute tutu. June and Ruby played a duet on their lutes. Duke played his huge tuba to end the show. Ruby said her friends were all super!

1. Color the picture. Look at the people in the picture.

2. Who did you color? _____

3. Who are the characters? _____

4. What is the setting, or where the story takes place? _____

5. What was the main event? _____

☐ **I can use pictures and details in a story to describe characters, settings, and events.**
☐ **I can read first-grade text.**

Name_____

Read the story.

A Tale of Two Mice

Once upon a time, two little mice lived happily. One mouse lived under a vine outside a large house. The other mouse lived under the tiles inside the large house.

The vine mouse liked to eat plain rice. The tile mouse liked to eat bites of fine food.

The vine mouse liked to play hide-and-seek outside. The tile mouse liked to sit inside.

The two mice were opposites. Still, the two mice were fine friends.

Fill in the chart. Write three facts about the vine mouse and the tile mouse.

Vine Mouse	Tile Mouse

☐ I can compare and contrast characters in a story.
☐ I can read first-grade text.

© Carson-Dellosa • CD-104608

24

Name_____

Read the story. Answer the questions.

Quiet Time

It's a time to read and a time to sleep.
It's a time to think and a time to weep.

It's a time to let your imagination run.
It's a time to plan how to get things done.

It's a time to sit and be alone.
   It's a time to be thankful for all you own.

   It's a time to watch a little ant.
      It's a time to say, "I can," not "I can't."

      It's a time to think about movies, books, and plays.
      It's a time to remember all your yesterdays.

      Quiet time is a special time but often overlooked.
      We forget to have some quiet time when we're
      overbooked.

1. Which sentence tells the main idea of the poem?
   A. Quiet time is boring.
   B. Quiet time is a special time for thinking.
   C. Quiet time is better than recess.

2. Pick the sentence that is not true about quiet time.
   A. Quiet time can be for reading.
   B. Quiet time is a good time to think.
   C. Quiet time is only at night when it is really quiet.

3. What do you like to do during quiet time? _____

_____

☐ **I can answer questions about text.**
☐ **I can read first-grade text.**

Name_____

Read the story. Answer the questions.

Playing Dress-Up

Allie likes to play dress-up. She likes
to dress as a bride. Allie will put on a
long white dress and drape a pretty
shawl on her head. She even has some
roses. Sometimes she will put on her big
sister's dance outfit. Then, she will do a
dance. Allie also thinks it is fun to be a
clown. She will put on her dad's shoes
and color her nose red.

Allie likes playing Mom best. She
dresses up in her mom's clothes. She
takes her bag and shops for food in the
kitchen pantry. Her doll is always her
baby. She feeds her baby. Then, she
sings her baby to sleep.

Playing dress-up is a lot of fun.

1. What is the main idea of this story?
   A. Allie likes to dress up as a bride.
   B. Playing dress-up is a lot of fun.
   C. Allie likes to dress up as a clown.

2. What does Allie like dressing up as best?
   A. Mom
   B. a dancer
   C. a clown

3. Who is your favorite person to dress up as? Why? _____

_____

☐ **I can answer questions about text.**
☐ **I can read first-grade text.**

26

© Carson-Dellosa • CD-104608

Read the poem. Answer the questions.

Colors All Around

Look for colors all around.
What colors of a rainbow can be found?

Green is found in the grasshopper hopping around the lake.
Brown is found in the syrup on my pancake.

Red is found in a superhero's cape.
Purple is found in a vineyard grape.
Blue is found in a blueberry pie.

Orange is found in a clown's bow tie.
Yellow is found in a sunflower.
Black is found at the midnight hour.

Colors of the rainbow can be found,
if you'll only take the time to look around.

1. What is the main idea of this poem?
   A. Rainbows are very pretty.
   B. Rainbows come out after the rain.
   C. Colors can be found all around us.

2. What is your favorite color? _____

3. Name three things that are the same color. _____

_____

☐ **I can read first-grade text.**

> Reading for details is being able to find specific answers to questions about text.

A Tasty Butterfly

Butterflies are lovely to look at, but here is how to make one you can eat!

You will need:

- 2 frozen pancakes
- 1 banana
- 2 grapes

- 2 pieces of link sausage
- 2 toothpicks
- jelly

Here is how to make it:

- Toast the pancakes and cut them in half. This will make the four pieces you will need for the four wings of the butterfly.
- Peel the banana and place it on the plate. This will be the butterfly's body.
- Place the cut sides of the pancakes next to the banana to form the butterfly's wings.
- Spread jelly on the "wings."
- Use the toothpicks to hold the grapes on the banana as eyes.
- Cook the sausages and place them at the top of the banana as antennae.

Use details from the text to fill in the missing words.

1. The _____ will make the butterfly's body.

2. The wings will be covered with _____.

3. Butterflies have four _____.

4. The antennae will be made from _____.

5. A butterfly has two _____ to see with.

> ☐ **I can answer questions about key details in a text.**
> ☐ **I can read first-grade text.**

Each title tells a main idea. Write each title above the correct passage. Remember to ask yourself, "Does this title tell about the whole passage?"

The Water Cycle of the Dead Sea

What is the Dead Sea?

The Uses of the Dead Sea

The Salty Waters of the Dead Sea

1. _____

_____

The Dead Sea is a saltwater lake. It is in Asia. It is near Jordan and Israel. The lake is very deep. It is deeper at the north end. It is over 1000 feet below sea level. The south end of the Dead Sea is shallow.

2. _____

_____

The Dead Sea is much saltier than the ocean! The salt is very thick. No plants can grow in the water. No animals can live in the water. That is why it is called the Dead Sea. The salt is so thick that swimmers can float on top!

3. _____

_____

The Dead Sea is valuable. It is easy to get salt from it. People use the water for beauty and health. Some people go there to fix skin problems. Many people go to the Dead Sea for those reasons.

4. _____

_____

The Dead Sea gets water from the Jordan River. The river goes into the sea. Other small streams go into the Dead Sea too. No rivers lead out of the sea. The water stays in place. It gets very salty this way. The Dead Sea is in a desert, so it gets salty fast!

☐ **I can find the main idea by using key details.**
☐ **I can read first-grade text.**

Children on Farms

Children live on farms all over the world. These boys and girls learn about animals on the farm. Some children can milk a cow. Other children can feed the horses. Children on a farm may even help cut a sheep's wool!

Children on farms can learn about fruits and vegetables also. Boys and girls can help in the garden. They can pick apples from the apple trees. They can pick berries from the bushes. Some children can even plant the seeds by themselves! Living on a farm can be fun.

1. What is the main idea of the text? _____

_____

2. What can children do with animals on the farm? _____

_____

3. What can children do with fruits and vegetables on the farm? ____

_____

☐ I can find the main idea.
☐ I can answer questions about details in a text.
☐ I can read first-grade text.

Charts and tables are helpful in grouping information. To read the chart, match the given information from the top and the left side to find new information in the boxes.

Name	Test A	Test B	Test C
Haley	99	93	97
Michael	43	45	58
Robert	76	81	85
Danisha	98	76	88
Quan	25	76	89
Jamal	76	76	76
Monica	79	83	88
Kira	76	75	74

Use the chart to answer the questions.

1. Which three students had the same score on Test B?

_____   _____   _____

2. Who had the lowest score on Test C? _____

3. Who had the highest score on Test A? _____

4. What were Robert's scores on Tests A and C? _____

5. Who had the lowest score on Test A? _____

6. Which three students had the same score on Test A?

_____   _____   _____

☐ I can see the links between information in a text.
☐ I can locate facts in a text.

Read the text. Look at the bold words closely.

Hamsters

Hamsters are small animals. They were found in Syria hundreds of years ago. They live in many parts of the world. Hamsters like to **hoard**, or keep, food in their big cheeks. Their cheeks are like pouches. They store nuts and seeds inside. Hamsters are known to like to stay up at night. This means they are **nocturnal**. Some family members think hamsters are great pets. But hamsters like to **stay up very late**!

Answer the questions.

1. What does the word **hoard** mean? _____

_____

2. What does the word **nocturnal** mean? _____

_____

3. What does it mean to **stay up very late**? _____

_____

4. Choose a bold word or group of words. Write your own sentence using the

word or group of words. _____

_____

☐ **I can understand the meaning of words and phrases (groups of words) in a text.**
☐ **I can read first-grade text.**

> Charts and tables are helpful in organizing information. To read the chart, match the given information from the top and the left side to find new information in the boxes.

	Monday	**Tuesday**	**Wednesday**	**Thursday**	**Friday**
Reading	Sandie	Elena	Sam	Kendra	Evan
Listening	Elena	Sam	Kendra	Evan	Sandie
Math	Sam	Kendra	Evan	Sandie	Elena
Art	Kendra	Evan	Sandie	Elena	Sam
Science	Evan	Sandie	Elena	Sam	Kendra

Use the chart to answer the questions.

1. Who will use the art center on Thursday? _____

2. What center will Sam use on Monday? _____

3. On what day will Evan use the science center? _____

4. What center will Sandie use on Friday? _____

5. Who will use the reading center on Wednesday? _____

6. On what day will Elena use the math center? _____

❑ I can see the links between information in a text.
❑ I can locate facts in a text.

Pictures and text give information. Pictures give you clues about a topic. A passage, or text, also gives you facts about a topic.

Look at the pictures. What do you see? Write a fact under each one.

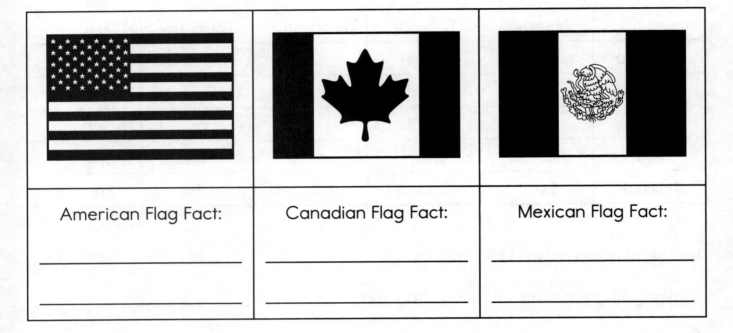

American Flag Fact:	Canadian Flag Fact:	Mexican Flag Fact:
_____	_____	_____
_____	_____	_____

The pictures give information. We can tell what the flags look like from the pictures. Read the flag facts below. Underline the color words.

The American flag has stripes. It is red, white, and blue. The American flag has stars.	The Canadian flag has a maple leaf. It is red and white. The leaf is red.	The Mexican flag has a bird. It is red, white, and green. The bird holds a snake.

☐ **I can use pictures and text to understand information.**

Graphs show information. We can compare more than one thing. A bar graph has bars or columns to show information.

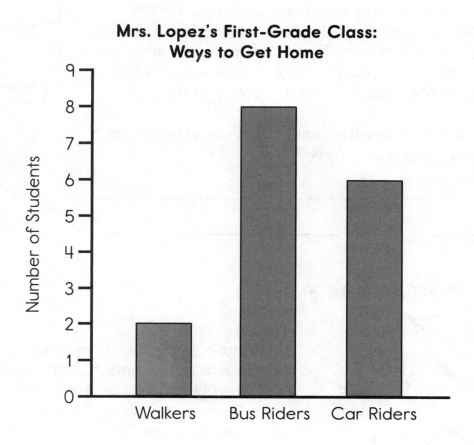

**Mrs. Lopez's First-Grade Class:
Ways to Get Home**

Use the bar graph to answer the questions.

1. How many students ride the bus home? _____

2. How many students walk home? _____

3. What is the title of the graph? _____

_____

4. Do more students take the bus or ride in a car? _____

☐ **I can use pictures to understand key ideas.**

Read the text. Answer the question.

Ice cream is the greatest dessert. I like to eat it after dinner. Sometimes, I eat one scoop. Other times, I have two scoops! I like to have chocolate ice cream. I also like mint chocolate chip ice cream. I like ice cream because it is sweet. I like ice cream because it cools me down on a hot day. When I go to the beach, I eat this cold treat!

1. The author is the writer. The author likes ice cream. What two reasons did the author give?

   _____

   _____

Read the text. Answer the question.

Sand castles are made of sand. I can build them at the beach. I can stack the sand castle up high. I mix water with the sand to help it stay together. I like sand castles because they are fun to build at the beach. I also like them because I can build them with friends. Sand castles are fun to build!

2. The author is the writer. The author likes sand castles. What two reasons did the author give?

   _____

   _____

☐ I can find reasons why the author feels a certain way about a topic.
☐ I can read first-grade text.

1.RI.10, 1.RF.4

Read the two passages. Fill in the chart on page 38.

The Man Who Never Lied
(An African Tale)

Once, long ago, a man named Mamad lived far away. He never told a lie. All of the people knew he was truthful. The king wanted to meet Mamad. "Mamad, will you ever tell a lie?" the king asked. "No, I will never tell a lie," Mamad said.

A few days later, the king called for Mamad again. He was ready to go hunting. "Mamad, will you tell the queen that I will join her for lunch this afternoon? Please tell her to cook a lot of food," the king said. "Yes, sir," Mamad said. Mamad left. The king laughed and decided not to go hunting and not to leave at all. He wanted Mamad to lie.

Mamad went to the queen. He was smart and said, "Queen, maybe you should make food for your king this afternoon. Maybe you should not. Maybe he will come this afternoon. But maybe not." The queen was confused!

The king told the people Mamad had lied to the queen. Then, the queen told them what Mamad said. The king knew Mamad was a wise man after that.

Mamad never told a lie.

Pinocchio
(An Italian Tale)

Many years ago, a man named Geppetto lived in a cottage. He wanted a son. He carved a boy out of wood. The puppet came to life!

Pinocchio the puppet ran away, but he soon came home. Geppetto took care of him and made him food. Geppetto asked where he had been. Pinocchio said he had gone to the park. His nose started to grow! Geppetto knew he was telling a lie. He told him not to do that.

Pinocchio went to school with kids. On his way, he heard music from a puppet show. He told his friends he would be at school soon. His nose started to grow again! He had told a lie. He joined the show and did not go to school.

The puppet master wanted to keep Pinocchio. He told the master he was going to get something. His nose started to grow! He had told a lie again. Pinocchio climbed a tree and started to go home.

Geppetto was worried. He looked for Pinocchio everywhere! He found him and asked where he had been. Pinocchio told Geppetto the whole story. His nose went back to normal. He had learned not to lie.

☐ **I can read first-grade text.**

The tale of Mamad and the tale of Pinocchio are two very similar but different stories. Fill in the chart.

What was similar between Mamad and Pinocchio?	What was different about Mamad and Pinocchio?
_____	_____
_____	_____
_____	_____
_____	_____
_____	_____
_____	_____

1. What did the king learn from Mamad? _____

_____

2. What did Pinocchio learn from Geppetto? _____

_____

3. How do you feel about people who tell lies? _____

_____

- ☐ **I can read first-grade text.**
- ☐ **I can find similarities and differences between two texts.**

A **fact** is something you know is true. An **opinion** is what you believe about something.

Gorillas

Gorillas live in the mountains and in the forests. Many gorillas live in Africa. They are peaceful animals, so scientists study them. They found that gorillas live in groups. The groups have males, females, and babies. Each group has one leader. A baby gorilla does not live with its mother for long enough. After about three years, it is on its own. At night, gorillas build nests to sleep in. They pick leaves and lie on them. Gorillas eat many foods. They like fruits, leaves, and juicy stems. Gorillas are almost extinct. Their forests are being destroyed. We should help save their forests.

Write three facts from the passage.

1. _____

2. _____

3. _____

Write three opinions from the passage.

1. _____

2. _____

3. _____

☐ **I can read first-grade text.**

Read each text aloud to a classmate. Your classmate will fill out the chart next to each text.

Hint: The name "Hsing" is said like the word "Sing."

Brenda Morgan, a zookeeper has an important job. She takes care of animals. She once took care of a panda named Hsing-Hsing. Brenda took care of Hsing-Hsing like a mother takes care of a child.

Did the reader say the words right? yes   no

Which words did the reader miss?

_____

Did the reader read too fast or too slow? yes   no

Did the reader show feeling? yes   no

Part of Brenda's job was to watch Hsing-Hsing closely. She had to be sure he felt well. Once, he had an eye problem. He could not see. Brenda called the vet. Hsing-Hsing got medicine and felt better. Soon, he was well again.

Did the reader say the words right? yes   no

Which words did the reader miss?

_____

Did the reader read too fast or too slow? yes   no

Did the reader show feeling? yes   no

Hsing-Hsing ate many foods. He liked rice, honey, and sweet potatoes. He also liked apples and bamboo. Brenda thought his favorite food was carrots. She fed him every day at the zoo.

Did the reader say the words right? yes   no

Which words did the reader miss?

_____

Did the reader read too fast or too slow? yes   no

Did the reader show feeling? yes   no

☐ I can read and understand an organized text.
☐ I can read aloud correctly, fluently, and with feeling.

> The first word of a sentence begins with an uppercase letter.
>
> Example: <u>S</u>ome birds are different.

Write *yes* if the sentence is written correctly. Write *no* if it is not.

1. _____ What is a kea?

2. _____ a kea is a bird.

3. _____ It is a kind of parrot.

4. _____ where do keas live?

5. _____ They live in New Zealand.

6. _____ they are green.

7. _____ keas eat bugs and fruit.

8. Choose a sentence above that was not written correctly. Write it correctly on the lines.

_____

_____

☐ **I can recognize sentence features.**
☐ **I can capitalize the first word of a sentence.**

A **syllable** is a word part. Each syllable has a vowel sound.

Say each word aloud. Count the number of syllables in each word. Write the number on the line.

1. horse _____

2. chair _____

3. oven _____

4. sister _____

5. bookcase _____

6. robot _____

7. kitchen _____

8. yesterday _____

9. bird _____

10. bicycle _____

Look around your classroom. Write words in the boxes below. Count the syllables for each word.

Classroom Items	Number of Syllables

☐ **I can understand spoken words and syllables.**
☐ **I can hear vowel sounds and count syllables.**

When words have the same ending sounds and rhyme, these words belong in the same **word family**.

Examples: b<u>and</u>, h<u>and</u>, l<u>and</u>

Read each word. Look at the underlined word ending. Then, write as many words as you can for each word family.

r<u>at</u>	T<u>im</u>	k<u>it</u>
r<u>ate</u>	**t<u>ime</u>**	**k<u>ite</u>**

☐ I can hear short vowel sounds in words.
☐ I can hear long vowel sounds in words.

The words below have a beginning sound, a middle sound, and an ending sound. Say the words aloud. Break the words apart by sound. Place each sound in the box next to the word.

Word	Beginning Sound	Middle Sound	Ending Sound
bun			
hip			
get			
sun			
bat			

Some words start with two consonants. Consonant blends have two consonants, and each makes one sound.

Example: sw in <u>sw</u>im

Say the words aloud. Break the words apart by sound. Place each sound in the box next to the word. Remember blends count as two sounds!

Blend Word	Beginning Blend Sound 1	Beginning Blend Sound 2	Middle Sound	Ending Sound
flip				
brim				
swap				
slim				
grip				

☐ I can blend the sounds of a word.
☐ I can say the first, second, and last sounds in a single syllable word.

Answer the questions. Be sure to say each word aloud. Listen to each sound as you say the word. Think of what letter stands for each sound.

1. What is the first sound in the word *fish?* _____

2. What is the second sound in the word *hot?* _____

3. What is the last sound in the word *goat?* _____

4. What is the first sound in the word *went?* _____

5. What is the second sound in the word *yes?* _____

6. What is the last sound in the word *dad?* _____

7. What is the first sound in the word *golf?* _____

8. What is the second sound in the word *fan?* _____

9. What is the last sound in the word *sat?* _____

10. What is the first sound in the word *kite?* _____

11. Say your name aloud. What is the first sound? _____

12. Say your teacher's name. What is the last sound of your teacher's last name?

_____

☐ **I can say the first, second, and last sounds in a single syllable word.**
☐ **I can find sounds in a word.**

1.RF.2d

Each word below has one syllable. Each word has a beginning sound, a middle sound, and an ending sound. The middle sound is a vowel sound. Write the correct sound on the line. A letter stands for a sound.

Beginning Sound	 1. ___og	 2. ___an
	 3. ___op	 4. ___en
Middle Sound	 5. c___t	 6. j___g
	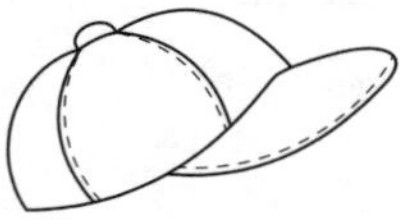 7. c___p	 8. j___t
Ending Sound	 9. lo___	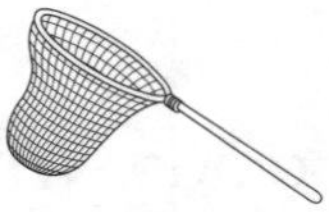 10. ne___
	 11. ca___	 12. ba___

☐ **I can break apart words by sound.**
☐ **I can understand that each letter stands for a sound.**

© Carson-Dellosa • CD-104608

Words that rhyme sound alike. Follow the directions below. You will need crayons!

1. Find two pictures that rhyme with *snake*. Color them green.
2. Draw a blue triangle around each picture that rhymes with *stone*.
3. Use black to cross out the pictures in the top row that rhyme with *lie*.
4. Find two pictures that rhyme with *wire*. Color them red.
5. Draw a brown circle around each picture that rhymes with *plate*.

☐ **I can decode words.**

All words have word parts called syllables. The number of syllables in a word is the same number of vowel sounds you hear in the word.

Examples: dog = one syllable and one vowel sound
zebra = two syllables and two vowel sounds

Say these words. Separate the words into syllables as you write the letters in the boxes. Tell how many syllables each word has.

1. apartment

_____

2. interesting

_____

3. enormous

_____

4. subtraction

_____

5. individual

_____

6. fascination

_____

7. amphibian

_____

8. intelligent

_____

☐ **I can decode words.**

Consonant blends are two consonant letters next to each other at the beginning or the end of a word. Each letter makes its own sound.

Examples: *sn* in <u>sn</u>eeze, *tr* in <u>tr</u>ip, *sl* in <u>sl</u>ow, *cl* in <u>cl</u>own

Consonant digraphs are two consonant letters next to each other at the beginning or the end of a word. Together, both letters make one sound.

Examples: *sh* in <u>sh</u>ip, *ch* in pit<u>ch</u>, *ck* in sock, *th* in <u>th</u>in,

Decide what consonant blend is missing in each word and write the letters on the lines.

 1. ____ ____ee

 2. ____ ____ed

 3. ____ ____oud

 4. ____ ____ake

Decide what consonant digraph is missing in each word and write the letters on the lines.

 5. cat ____ ____

 6. ____ ____ip

 7. wi ____ ____

 8. ____ ____umb

☐ **I can understand words with consonant blends and digraphs.**

Name_____

1.RF.3a

Find a word in the word bank that begins with the same sound as each picture.
Write the word above the picture.

black	clap	chipmunk	floor
glare	shoe	sky	sled
stamp	thin	train	whirl

1.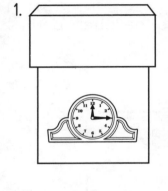

2.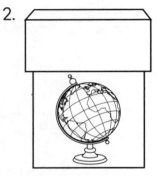

3.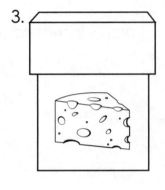

4.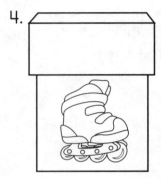

5.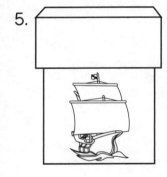

6.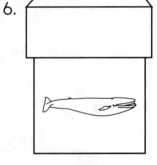

7.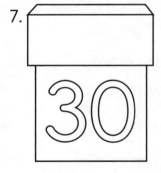

8.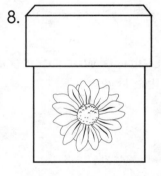

9.

10.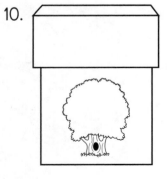

11.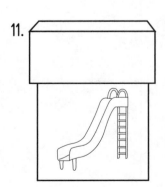

12.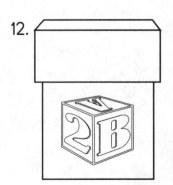

☐ **I can understand words with consonant blends and digraphs.**

50

© Carson-Dellosa • CD-104608

Write the correct consonant blend or digraph to complete the missing word in each sentence.

bank	cement	couch	lungs	months	pink
sand	scold	sprint	squash	trend	wing

1. A wi____ ____ is one of the moveable, feathered parts a bird uses to fly.

2. A ba____ ____ is a place to hold money.

3. Sa____ ____ is often found at a beach.

4. If you sco____ ____ someone, you correct that person.

5. Ceme____ ____ is a hard material used to make sidewalks and buildings.

6. Cou____ ____ means the same as sofa.

7. A tre____ ____ is a fad in clothing and toys.

8. Twelve mon____ ____s are in a year.

9. If you spri____ ____, you quickly run a short distance.

10. The lu____ ____s are part of the human body.

11. Pi____ ____ is the color of bubble gum.

12. Butternut is a type of squa____ ____.

☐ **I can understand words with consonant blends and digraphs.**

Name_____

Each syllable in a word has one vowel sound. Use the word families to make one-syllable words. You may use each word family more than once. Do not repeat any words.

and	ank	ash	ent	est	ick	ing
ish	ock	old	ong	ung	unk	ust

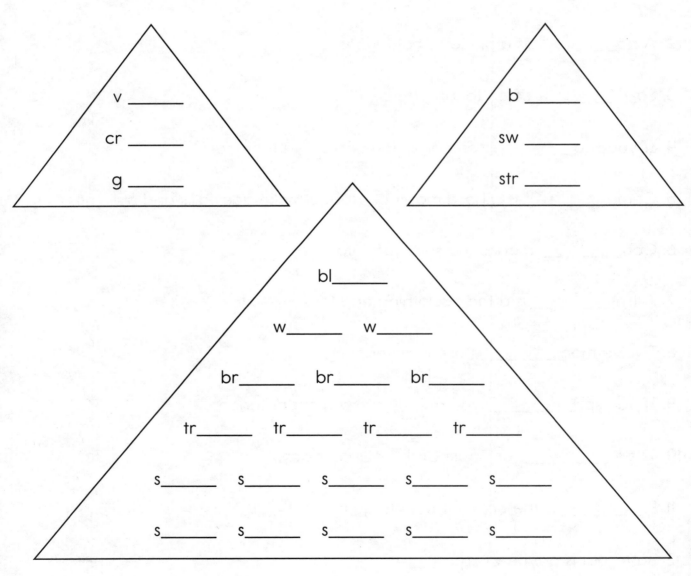

v _____

cr _____

g _____

b _____

sw _____

str _____

bl_____

w_____   w_____

br_____   br_____   br_____

tr_____   tr_____   tr_____   tr_____

s_____   s_____   s_____   s_____   s_____

s_____   s_____   s_____   s_____   s_____

☐ **I can decode one-syllable words.**

When **y** comes at the end of a word, it is a vowel. When **y** comes at the end of a one-syllable word, it makes the **long i sound**.

Examples: my, fry, dry

Use the words in the word bank to answer the questions or to fill in the blanks.

fly	my	sky	try	why

1. Which word means *something belongs to me?* _____

2. Which word asks a question? _____

3. The bird would fly way up in the _____.

4. I'm really shy, but I will _____.

5. No matter how I try, I cannot seem to _____.

6. Read each word and draw a picture.

sky	fly	cry

☐ **I can decode one-syllable words.**

> When a letter sounds like its name, it makes a long vowel sound.
>
> Examples: <u>a</u> in l<u>a</u>ke, <u>i</u> in h<u>i</u>ke
>
> When a word has a consonant-vowel-consonant-*e* pattern (CVCe), the vowel sound is usually long, and the *e* is silent.
>
> Examples: name, ride, note, cute

Complete the word at the end of each sentence. Then, find and circle each answer in the word search. Words appear down, diagonally, or backward.

1. A gorilla is a kind of a____ ____.

2. A dog likes to chew on a b____ ____ ____.

3. On a windy day, you can fly a k____ ____ ____.

4. People laugh when they are told a funny j____ ____ ____.

5. You squeeze toothpaste out of a t____ ____ ____.

6. Food is served on a p____ ____ ____ ____.

7. If you are not afraid, you are b____ ____ ____ ____.

8. If you win a game, you sometimes get a p____ ____ ____ ____.

```
r  w  p  e  m  l  f  q  e  r
q  g  n  p  g  o  l  r  e  z
f  o  j  r  v  a  c  b  p  p
b  j  o  i  q  t  u  h  l  e
d  g  k  z  i  t  u  a  a  j
s  t  e  e  j  b  o  b  t  e
j  b  m  i  p  r  c  z  e  k
c  a  j  n  r  a  u  q  s  i
h  x  p  g  e  v  b  j  d  t
u  k  g  e  y  e  e  s  o  e
```

☐ **I can understand long vowel sounds and rules.**

Name_____

Vowel teams are two vowel letters next to each other that usually make one sound. The vowel teams **ai**, **ea**, **ee**, and **oa** often make a long vowel sound.

Examples: w<u>ai</u>t, r<u>ea</u>l, b<u>ee</u>, g<u>oa</u>t

Read each clue. Then, complete each word with the correct vowel team.

1. What do you do when you are tired?

    sl _____ _____ p

2. This is water that falls from the sky.

    r _____ _____ n

3. You use this in a bath.

    s _____ _____ p

4. Jack carried this up a hill.

    p _____ _____ l

5. You ride in this on water.

    b _____ _____ t

6. You play in the sand here.

    b _____ _____ ch

7. You do this with your eyes.

    s _____ _____

☐ **I can understand long vowel sounds and rules.**

Find out how many syllables are in each word. Say each word. Count the number of vowels you hear. Write the number on the line.

1. dragon _____

2. frog _____

3. itch _____

4. peanut _____

5. potato _____

6. watermelon _____

7. camera _____

8. hero _____

9. Tyrannosaurus _____

10. journal _____

Look at the words in the word bank. Answer the questions.

| hippopotamus | starfish | tarantula | yard |

11. Which word has five syllables? _____

12. How many syllables does *starfish* have? _____

13. Which word has only one syllable? _____

14. How many syllables does tarantula have? _____

☐ **I can use syllable rules to find the number of syllables in a word.**

Name_____

A compound word is a word made up of two or more words together. The joined words make a new word with a new meaning.

Example: butter + fly = butterfly

Use words in the word bank to form a two-syllable compound word. Each word will become a two-syllable compound word.

air	ball	fire	house
road	sea	stick	suds

1.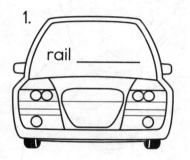
rail _____

2.
drum _____

3.
soap _____

4.
_____ plane

5.
_____ shell

6.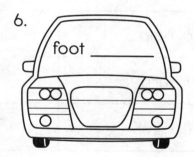
foot _____

7.
_____ works

8.
play _____

☐ I can understand compound words.
☐ I can decode two-syllable words.

Verbs are action words. Verbs can have an ending that shows they were an action done in the past. The ending is -ed.

Example: Today I yell for Mom. Yesterday I yell**ed** for Mom.

Look at the verbs below. Write the verb with -ed on the end of the word to show it was done yesterday.

Today, I...	Yesterday, I...
1. pull	
2. pick	
3. ask	
4. want	
5. look	
6. help	
7. turn	
8. climb	

What if you do something tomorrow? Use an extra verb, will. Pick two verbs and complete the sentences.

9. I will _____ .

10. I will _____ .

☐ **I understand many verbs that end in -ed show an action done in the past.**
☐ **I can understand past and future verbs.**

Verbs are action words. Verbs can have an ending that shows they are an action happening now. The ending is -ing.

Example: Sometimes I find my toys. Right now I am find<u>ing</u> my toys.

Look at the verbs below. Write the verb with -ing on the end of the word to show it is being done right now.

Sometimes, I...	Right now, I am...
1. talk	
2. sleep	
3. watch	
4. cook	
5. cry	
6. clean	
7. jump	
8. mix	

What if you do something tomorrow? You use an extra verb, will. Use a verb from above and complete the sentence.

9. I will _____ .

10. I will _____ .

☐ **I understand many verbs that end in -ing show an action happening now.**
☐ **I can understand present and future verbs.**

Some words are not spelled the way the rules tell you to spell them. These words are called **irregular** words. They have their own spelling.

Example: The word *was* sounds like it should be spelled *wuz*.

Read the irregular words aloud. Write a sentence next to each one.

Irregular Word	Sentence
1. they	
2. your	
3. because	
4. enough	
5. were	
6. one	
7. people	
8. know	

❑ **I can read first-grade irregular words.**

Some words are not spelled the way the rules tell you to spell them. These words are called **irregular** words. They have their own spelling.

Example: The word *does* sounds like it should be spelled *duz*.

Read the irregular words aloud. Write a sentence next to each one.

Irregular Word	Sentence
1. should	
2. two	
3. there	
4. said	
5. who	
6. come	
7. again	
8. off	

☐ I can read first-grade irregular words.

Look at the clock. Write down the time you start to read. Read the text. Look at the clock when you are done. Write the time. Answer the questions.

Start Time: _____

Wave Rider

Nate has a sailboat named *Wave Rider*. James is Nate's shipmate. Nate sails the boat. James keeps the boat clean and neat.

Nate and James like to sail whenever they can. Today, they catch a big wave out to sea. Nate brags about the perfect day. Suddenly, it starts to rain.

The sea is no longer safe. The wind seems to scream, "Race to shore!" James and Nate sail the boat back to shore. They will wait for another day.

End Time: _____

1. Did you read all of the words with ease? _____

2. Which words were hard to read? _____

3. How long did it take you to read the 80 words in *Wave Rider*? _____

Read the passage one more time. Write down your start and end times below.

Start Time: _____

End Time: _____

4. Did you read all of the words? _____

5. Which words were hard to read? _____

6. How long did it take you to read the text the second time? _____

☐ **I can read a first-grade text with accuracy and fluency.**

Some words are spelled alike and sound alike, but they have different meanings. We know which meaning makes sense by reading the rest of the sentence.

Example: I turned the <u>fan</u> on to cool off the room.
The <u>fan</u> cheered for the football team.

Read each pair of sentences. Write the word from the word bank that makes sense in both sentences. Reread the sentences if you need to.

back	fall	roll	saw	star

1. Matt _____ a lion at the zoo.

   Dad cut the tree with a _____.

2. Leaves change colors in the _____.

   Raindrops _____ from the sky.

3. Jan was the _____ of the show.

   She drew a _____ on her paper.

4. I ate a _____ at lunch.

   Sam will _____ the ball to her.

5. Ann shut the _____ door.

   Tim swam on his _____.

☐ I can use context to understand which words to use.
☐ I can reread text if I need to.
☐ I can figure out the meanings of words.

Sometimes, you want the reader to agree with what you think. You want them to agree with your opinion. Your opinion shows how you feel about a topic.

Think about this question: Should students get 30 minutes of free time at school each day?

Answer the questions.

1. What is your opinion? Write two sentences.

_____

_____

2. Who are you trying to persuade? Why? Write two sentences.

_____

_____

3. Why should others agree with you? List two reasons that support your opinion.

A. _____

B. _____

4. Write an ending sentence for your opinion.

Finally, others should agree with me because _____

_____

_____ .

☐ **I can write an opinion on a topic, give reasons for the opinion, and give a closing sentence.**

Sometimes, you want the reader to agree with what you think. You want them to agree with your opinion. Your opinion shows how you feel about a topic.

Think about this question: Should students ask the principal for new computers for your classroom?

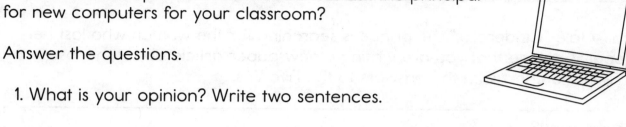

Answer the questions.

1. What is your opinion? Write two sentences.

_____

_____

2. Who are you trying to persuade? Why? Write two sentences.

_____

_____

3. Why should others agree with you? List two reasons that support your opinion.

A. _____

B. _____

4. Write an ending sentence for your opinion.

Finally, others should agree with me because _____

_____

_____.

❑ **I can write an opinion on a topic, give reasons for the opinion, and give a closing sentence.**

Most newspaper and magazine articles include the **Five W's**: What happened? Who was there? When did it happen? Where did it happen? Why did it happen? When you write a news article, it is important to include this information.

In the fairy tale "Cinderella," the prince is searching for the woman who lost her glass slipper. Imagine that you are writing a newspaper article about the lost slipper. Fill in the chart with the answers to the Five W's.

What happened?	
Who was there?	
When did it happen?	
Where did it happen?	
Why did it happen?	

- ☐ **I can write informative texts about a topic and give facts about it.**
- ☐ **I can make good choices when writing.**

You can use facts, reasons, and examples to explain topics in your writing. A topic is what you write about.

Read the prompt. Use the charts to help you write about your favorite subject.

Topic

My favorite subject is _____.

Why is it your favorite?
Give a reason.

_____

_____

_____

Why is it your favorite?
Give another reason.

_____

_____

_____

Tell me more! Give an example.

_____

_____

_____

Tell me more! Give an example.

_____

_____

_____

Ending

_____

_____

_____

☐ **I can write informative texts about a topic and give facts about it.**
☐ **I can provide a sense of closure.**

Name_____

Think about a special event in your life. Fill in the chart with answers to the
Five W's.

What happened?
Who was there?
When did it happen?
Where did it happen?
Why did it happen?

☐ **I can write about an event in my life.**

Journal writing is a way to share ideas, thoughts, and feelings. It helps to start your sentences with time-order words, such as *first*, *then*, *after*, and *finally*. It gives your writing order.

Respond to the journal prompt.

What would you do if you were principal for the day?

First, _____ .

Then, _____ .

After, _____ .

Finally, _____ .

Draw a picture of yourself as principal!

☐ **I can write with time words.**
☐ **I can respond to a journal prompt.**

Name_____

> You can use facts and examples to explain a topic in your writing.
> A **topic** is what you write about.

1. Read the prompt.

   People like many kinds of food. Think about the food you like best. Explain why you like it.

2. Complete the chart. Use words to explain your topic.

| **Topic** |
| My favorite food is _____. |

Why do you like this food? Give a reason.	Why else do you like this food? Give another reason.
_____	_____
_____	_____

Tell me more! Give an example.	Tell me more! Give an example.
_____	_____
_____	_____

| **Ending** |
| _____ |

3. Share your writing with a classmate. Ask your classmate to make suggestions to fix your writing and to write a sentence about your writing below.

_____

☐ I can focus on a topic when I write.
☐ I can get writing help from a classmate.
☐ I can fix my writing.

You are going to write a story. In this story, a child will go ice-skating for the first time! The middle of the story has been written for you.

1. Write a beginning and an ending to finish the story.

Beginning
Middle   We put our ice skates on. We walked to the skating rink. I grabbed Mom's hand and looked at the other children. They were laughing and having a great time! I took a deep breath. I stepped onto the ice for the first time. My mom helped me balance. I placed one foot in front of the other.
End

2. Have a classmate look at your beginning and your ending. Ask your classmate to make suggestions about your writing. This can make your writing stronger. Your classmate can use the checklist below.

1. How can the writer make the beginning better?	
2. How can the writer make the ending better?	
3. What do you like about what your classmate wrote?	

- ☐ I can focus on a topic when I write.
- ☐ I can get writing help from a classmate.
- ☐ I can fix my writing.

Writers sometimes write about what happens in their lives. Things in your life may give you ideas for writing topics. A **topic** is the subject that you are writing about.

1. Draw a picture of a special time when you felt happy and excited.

2. Write three sentences to explain your drawing.

_____

_____

_____

3. Type the sentences on the computer. Print a copy of your writing.

❑ **I can publish my writing.**

Everyone has different likes and experiences. Write three lists based on your life.

Things I Can Do

1. _____

2. _____

3. _____

Games I Like to Play

1. _____

2. _____

3. _____

Places I Have Been

1. _____

2. _____

3. _____

Type one list on the computer. Print a copy.

☐ **I can publish my writing.**

1. Find a classmate.
2. Research the topic of winter. Look in books. Read winter websites from your teacher or librarian.
3. Share information with your classmate.
4. Complete the chart with details about winter.

Topic: Winter

Fact #1	**Example for Fact #1**
_____	_____
_____	_____
_____	_____

Fact #2	**Example for Fact #2**
_____	_____
_____	_____
_____	_____

Fact #3	**Example for Fact #3**
_____	_____
_____	_____
_____	_____

☐ **I can research a topic with a classmate.**

Respond to each journal prompt.

What is the nicest thing that someone has done for you?

_____

_____

_____

_____

What is the nicest thing that you have done for someone else?

_____

_____

_____

_____

☐ I can answer a question with writing.
☐ I can remember information from my experiences.

Name_____

Write the alphabet below.

Uppercase Letters

Lowercase Letters

A **noun** is a person, place, thing, or idea. A **plural noun** is more than one.

   Examples: toy = noun, toys = plural noun

A **verb** is an action word. A noun and a plural noun need an action.

Fill in the chart. Circle the correct verbs to finish the sentences.

Noun or Plural Noun	Verb Choices	End of the Sentence
1. The buildings	*is* or *are*	very tall.
2. Mother	*want* or *wants*	to go inside.
3. The teacher	*write* or *writes*	on the board.
4. Spike and Buddy	*eat* or *eats*	all of their dog food.
5. East School	*is* or *are*	in my state.

Check your answers. Read each sentence aloud. Make sure the sentences sound right.

- ☐ **I can print all uppercase and lowercase letters.**
- ☐ **I can match verbs with singular and plural nouns.**

A common **noun** names a person, place, thing, or idea.

  Examples: My <u>brother</u> set the <u>table</u> in the <u>dining room</u> with <u>love</u>.
    (person)   (place)   (thing)   (idea)

Write each common noun in the correct box below.

| bedroom | chair | dad | freedom |
| love | mother | school | swing |

Person	Place	Thing	Idea

A **proper noun** names a special person, place, or thing. It begins with a capital letter.

  Examples: <u>Timothy</u> lives in <u>Washington</u> with his dog <u>Ruffy</u>.
    (person)   (place)   (thing)

Write each proper noun in the correct box below.

| America | Casey | Florida |
| Friday | January | Mrs. Wu |

Person	Place	Thing

☐ I can name nouns and proper nouns.
☐ I can capitalize proper nouns.

An **adjective** is a word that describes a person, place, thing, or idea.

Examples: a <u>large</u> man, a <u>small</u> room, a <u>sunny</u> day

Look at each pair of adjectives. Circle the adjective that describes the picture.

1. furry   rough

2. loud   late

3. rainy   round

4. boring   bumpy

5. tough   tiny

6. silly   sandy

7. strong   soft

8. sweet   shiny

☐ **I can understand adjectives.**

A **conjunction** is a word that joins together two sentences to make one long sentence. Some conjunctions are **and**, **or**, and **but**.

Example: I like the red car, <u>and</u> I like the blue car.

Join the two sentences. Use the conjunctions in the box. You can use each more than once.

and	but	or

1. We're going to the fair, _____ we're going to the beach.

2. The beach is fun, _____ I like the rides at the fair.

3. I like to drive the small cars, _____ I like to wave at my mother.

4. She likes the games, _____ I love driving.

5. I'll pick the sports car, _____ I'll pick the truck.

6. The car is pretty, _____ the truck looks huge.

7. Maybe I can drive one, _____ then I can drive the other one.

8. I'll pick the red car, _____ I'll drive the blue truck later.

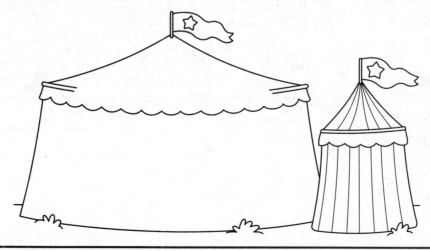

☐ **I can use conjunctions.**

A and **an** are special adjectives called **articles**. Use **a** to describe a singular noun that begins with a consonant sound. Use **an** to describe a singular noun that begins with a vowel or a vowel sound.

Examples: <u>a</u> coach, <u>an</u> ant

Write *a* or *an* in front of each noun.

1. _____ apple

2. _____ coconut

3. _____ banana

4. _____ zucchini

5. _____ orange

6. _____ pear

7. _____ eggplant

8. _____ pear

9. _____ pepper

10. _____ cherry

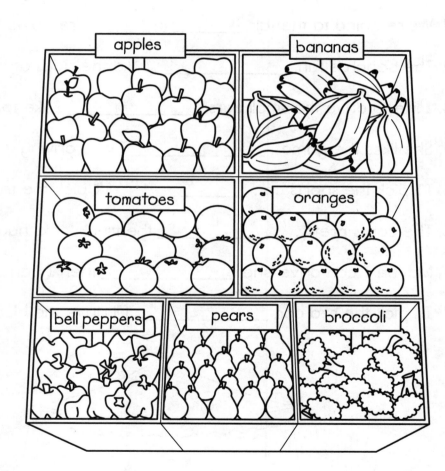

☐ **I can use the articles *a* and *an*.**

We use special words to show where something is. These words are called **prepositions**. They show where something is or what it is close to.

Use the prepositions in the box to complete the sentences.

at	in	on

1. I live _____ London.

2. The cat is _____ the table.

3. Sydney left the toy _____ her friend's house.

Use the prepositions in the box to complete the sentences.

across	around	behind

4. The puzzle piece was _____ the couch.

5. The necklace is _____ her neck.

6. I yelled _____ the lake to my friend.

Use the prepositions in the box to complete the sentences.

down	inside	over

7. We drove _____ the bridge.

8. It was time for dinner so Gus went _____ to eat.

9. She rode her bike _____ the hill.

☐ **I can use prepositions.**

Sentences come in four different types.

A **telling** sentence tells information. It ends with a period (**.**).

An **asking** sentence asks a question. It ends with a question mark (**?**).

An **exciting** sentence shows strong feelings. It ends with an exclamation point (**!**).

A **commanding** sentence gives an order. It ends with a period (**.**).

Identify the sentences. Write *T* for telling, *A* for asking, *E* for exciting, or *C* for commanding.

_____ 1. Do you have a new pet?

_____ 2. Yes, it was a birthday present!

_____ 3. What type of pet is it?

_____ 4. It is a beautiful calico kitten.

_____ 5. Wow, I have a calico kitten too!

_____ 6. Tell me about the cat.

_____ 7. She has a white belly.

_____ 8. Is she totally white?

_____ 9. No, she is black and brown.

_____ 10. Let me play with her.

☐ I can understand ending punctuation.
☐ I can understand different types of sentences.

These sentences are in trouble! They are missing a capital letter at the beginning. They have a word spelled wrong. And, no punctuation is at the end. Fix the sentences below. Write the fixed sentences.

1. elias was going to the stor

_____

2. henry felt very hapy

_____

3. would you take me to the lak

_____

4. can you se the big jet

_____

5. mother told me to eet my dinner

_____

Pronouns take the place of nouns.

    Example: <u>Mark</u> likes bikes. <u>He</u> likes bikes.

Use the word bank below. Replace the nouns with pronouns.

he	it	she	they	we

6. <u>Todd and I</u> will go to the mall. _____

7. <u>Grandma</u> will meet us there. _____

8. <u>Todd</u> wants to buy a shirt. _____

9. <u>The shirt</u> has to be blue. _____

10. <u>Grandma and Todd</u> will make sure it is the right size. _____

☐ **I can write sentences correctly.**
☐ **I can use pronouns.**

Use a comma (,) to separate a series of three or more things in a sentence.

Example: Juan has juice, yogurt, and carrots for his snack today.

Read the sentences. Add commas to separate three or more things in a series.

1. Rana bought eggs flour and butter to bake a cake.

2. Dad bought salad pears and bread at the grocery store.

3. I sit next to Joannie Grace and Sam in class.

4. My mom drives a yellow black and gray car.

5. The sandwich had turkey tomato and lettuce on wheat bread.

6. On vacation, Ned bought games puzzles and cards.

7. At the zoo, the children saw lions elephants and tigers.

8. We will need balloons cake and streamers for the party.

Use a comma to separate the day from the year when writing the date.

Example: March 24, 2013

9. February 4 2010

10. November 12 2014

☐ **I can use a comma to separate words in a series and in dates.**

A **prefix** is a word part that is at the beginning of some words. A prefix gives a clue to a word's meaning.

>   Example: <u>Re</u>do means to do something again. The prefix *re-* means *again*.

Use the prefixes in the box. Fill in the blanks. Then, write what the word means on the line.

pre-	**re-**	**un-**
before	again	not

1. _____view means to _____ .

2. _____tie means to _____ .

3. _____take means to _____ .

A **suffix** is a word part that is at the end of some words. A suffix gives a clue to a word's meaning.

>   Example: Care<u>less</u> is to do something without care. The suffix *-less* means *without*.

Use the suffixes in the box. Fill in the blanks. Then, write what the word means on the line.

-able	**-ful**	**-less**
able to	full of	without

4. Rest_____ means _____ .

5. Help_____ means _____ .

6. Build_____ means _____ .

☐ **I can use prefixes and suffixes to figure out what a word means.**

Words can be sorted into groups. These groups are called categories. **Categories** show what things some words may have in common.

Example: Turkey, ham, and beef are all types of meat.

Sort the words in the word bank into the groups.

apple	banana	bowl
coat	dish	fork
glove	hat	orange
pear	scarf	spoon

Fruits We Eat	Things We Wear in Cold Weather	Things We Use to Eat With

☐ I can sort words into groups (categories).

Name_____

Words can be sorted into groups. These groups are called categories.
Categories show what things some words may have in common.

Example: Circles, squares, and triangles are all types of shapes.

Sort the words in the word bank into the groups.

bobcat	duck	goose
iguana	jaguar	lion
lizard	penguin	snake
swan	tiger	turtle

Birds That Swim	Large Cats	Green Reptiles

☐ **I can sort words into groups (categories).**

Name_____

Words can be sorted into groups. These groups are called categories.
Categories show what things some words may have in common.

Example: Dolls, teddy bears, and blocks are all types of toys.

Sort the words in the word bank into the groups.

bike	broccoli	car
chocolate	cucumber	lettuce
mint	peas	skateboard
strawberry	tricycle	vanilla

Green Vegetables	Things with Wheels	Ice-Cream Flavors

☐ **I can sort words into groups (categories).**

Words have shades of meaning. They can mean almost the same thing but make the reader think different things. Think about how the underlined words are the same and different.

   Drew <u>sipped</u> his water.
   Drew <u>gulped</u> his water.

Find a partner. Act out each word below. Have fun!

1. walk	march	prance
2. whisper	talk	shout
3. look	stare	glance
4. pat	tap	poke
5. jump	skip	hop
6. cool	chilly	freezing
7. warm	hot	boiling
8. touch	grab	snatch

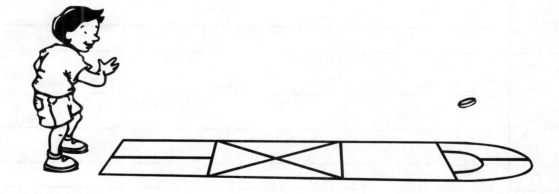

☐ **I can show that I understand shades of meaning by acting out the meaning of a word.**

Read the story.

Aunt Jill

Everyone can have a **special** person in their life.
The special person can be a friend or family member.
Pets can be special too! Aunt Jill is my special person.
She likes to draw pictures. She uses **different** colors.
She plays the piano. Aunt Jill bakes cookies in the oven.
She eats peanut butter cookies. Aunt Jill's **smile** makes
her special. She is always laughing. She is very happy.
She is my special person.

Write a sentence for each word from the story.

Word	Sentence
special	
different	
smile	

☐ **I can use words I found in a text I read.**

Answer Key

Page 12
1. C; 2. A; 3. A

Page 13
1. mother-tape, father-rope, sister-dime, brother-kite; 2. B; 3. B

Page 14
1. C; 2. B; 3. Answers will vary. 4. Answers will vary.

Page 15
1. Little Toad wants to find a home. Setting drawings may include a pond, old tree, or honey tree. Character drawings may include Little Toad, rabbit, bee, dog, or other toads.

Page 16
1. Billy and Katie decide to do nothing. Setting drawings may include an apple tree.

Page 17
1. Answers will vary but may include *still feeling weak* or *my dear*. 2. Answers will vary. 3. Answers will vary.

Page 18
1. Answers will vary but may include *I love spring, I like to sing, I wish I were a bird*, or *I feel like a king*. 2. Answers will vary. 3. Answers will vary.

Page 19
1. Fact; 2. Story; 3. Fact; 4. Fact; 5. Story; 6. Answers will vary. 7. Answers will vary. 8. Answers will vary.

Page 20
Books in the chart will vary. 1. A fiction book is a story, and a nonfiction book is facts. 2. Answers will vary.

Page 21
1. Sammy Snail, Robby Rabbit, Kami Kangaroo; 2. Robby Rabbit; 3. Kami Kangaroo; 4. Answers will vary but should not be any of the quotes.

Page 22
2. Answers will vary. 3. Mary, Mom, Dad; 4. Mary's house; 5. Mary made breakfast for Mom and Dad.

Page 23
2. Answers will vary. 3. Ruby, Judy, Hugo, Luke, Susan, June, Duke; 4. It takes place at the music show. 5. Ruby and her friends put on a music show.

Page 24
Vine Mouse: lived under a vine outside a large house, liked to eat plain rice, liked to play hide-and-seek outside.

Tile Mouse: lived under the tiles inside the large house, liked to eat bites of fine food, liked to sit inside.

Page 25
1. B; 2. C; 3. Answers will vary.

Page 26
1. B; 2. A; 3. Answers will vary.

Page 27
1. C; 2. Answers will vary. 3. Answers will vary.

Page 28
1. banana; 2. jelly; 3. wings; 4. sausage; 5. eyes

Page 29
1. The Dead Sea; 2. The Salty Waters of the Dead Sea; 3. The Uses of the Dead Sea; 4. The Water Cycle of the Dead Sea

Page 30
1. Children live on farms. 2. They can take care of the animals (milk, feed, or cut wool). 3. They can pick them.

Page 31
1. Danisha, Quan, Jamal; 2. Michael; 3. Haley; 4. 76, 85; 5. Quan; 6. Robert, Jamal, Kira

Page 32
1. *Hoard* means to keep or store. 2. *Nocturnal* means to be up at night. 3. To stay up very late is to be awake in the nighttime. 4. Answers will vary.

Page 33
1. Elena; 2. Math; 3. Monday; 4. Listening; 5. Sam; 6. Friday

Page 34
Flag answers vary based on student perception of flags (colors, symbols) and research.

Flag color words include: red, white, blue for the American flag; red and white for the Canadian flag; and red, white, and green for the Mexican flag.

Page 35
1. 8; 2. 2; 3. Mrs. Lopez's First-Grade Class: Ways to Get Home; 4. bus

Answer Key

Page 36
1. It is sweet, and it cools the author down on a hot day.
2. They are fun to build at the beach and with friends.

Page 38
Similar: Both stories are about lies and what can happen when a person lies.

Different: Mamad always told the truth, and Pinocchio lied. Mamad is in Africa, and Pinocchio is in Italy.

1. The king learned Mamad is honest and wise. 2. Pinocchio learned it is bad to lie. 3. Answers will vary.

Page 39
Facts: Gorillas live in the mountains and forests in Africa. Scientists study them. They live in groups. The groups have females, babies, and males. Gorillas build nests to sleep in. They eat foods like fruit, leaves and stems.

Opinions: They are peaceful and kind animals. Babies do not stay with their moms long enough. Stems are juicy and delicious. We should help save their forests.

Page 41
1. yes; 2. no; 3. yes; 4. no; 5. yes; 6. no; 7. no; 8. Answers will vary.

Page 42
1. 1; 2. 1; 3. 2; 4. 2; 5. 2; 6. 2; 7. 2; 8. 3; 9. 1; 10. 3; Chart: Answers will vary.

Page 43
Answers will vary but may include:

rat: bat, cat, fat, hat, mat, Nat, pat, sat

Tim: him, Jim, Kim, rim, swim, whim

kit: bit, fit, hit, lit, mitt, sit, wit

rate: bate, date, fate, gate, late, Kate, Nate

time: dime, grime, lime, mime, rhyme

kite: bite, mite, quite, site, white, write

Page 44

Word	Beginning Sound	Middle Sound	Ending Sound
bun	b	u	n
hip	h	i	p
get	g	e	t
sun	s	u	n
bat	b	a	t

Blend Word	Beginning Blend Sound 1	Beginning Blend Sound 2	Middle Sound	Ending Sound
flip	f	l	i	p
brim	b	r	i	m
swap	s	w	a	p
slim	s	l	i	m
grip	g	r	i	p

Page 45
1. f; 2. o; 3. t; 4. w; 5. e; 6. d; 7. g; 8. a; 9. t; 10. k; 11. Answers will vary. 12. Answers will vary.

Page 46
1. d; 2. p; 3. m; 4. p; 5. a; 6. u; 7. a; 8. e; 9. g; 10. t; 11. n; 12. t

Page 47
1. cake, rake; 2. bone, cone; 3. tie; 4. tire, fire; 5. skate, gate

Page 48

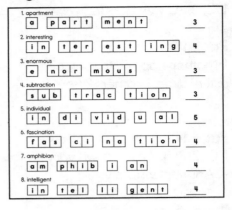

Page 49
1. tr; 2. sl; 3. cl; 4. sn; 5. ch; 6. sh; 7. sh; 8. th

Page 50
1. clever; 2. glare; 3. chipmunk; 4. sky; 5. shoe; 6. whirl; 7. this; 8. floor

Page 51
1. ng; 2. nk; 3. nd; 4. ld; 5. nt; 6. ch; 7. nd; 8. th; 9. nt; 10. ng; 11. nk; 12. sh

Page 52
Answers will vary.

Page 53
1. my; 2. why; 3. sky; 4. try; 5. fly; 6. Pictures will vary.

Page 54
1. ape; 2. bone; 3. kite; 4. joke; 5. tube; 6. plate; 7. brave; 8. prize

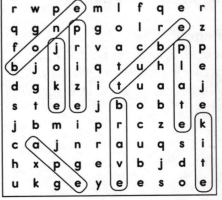

Answer Key

Page 55
1. sl<u>ee</u>p; 2. r<u>ai</u>n; 3. s<u>oa</u>p; 4. p<u>ai</u>l;
5. b<u>oa</u>t; 6. b<u>ea</u>ch; 7. s<u>ee</u>

Page 56
1. 2; 2. 1; 3. 1; 4. 2; 5. 3; 6. 4; 7. 3;
8. 2; 9. 5; 10. 2; 11. hippopotamus;
12. 2; 13. yard; 14. 4

Page 57
1. rail<u>road</u>; 2. drum<u>stick</u>;
3. soap<u>suds</u>; 4. <u>air</u>plane;
5. <u>sea</u>shell; 6. foot<u>ball</u>;
7. <u>fire</u>works; 8. play<u>house</u>

Page 58
1. pulled; 2. picked; 3. asked;
4. wanted; 5. looked; 6. helped;
7. turned; 8. climbed; 9. Answers
will vary. 10. Answers will vary.

Page 59
1. talking; 2. sleeping; 3. watching;
4. cooking; 5. crying; 6. cleaning;
7. jumping; 8. mixing; 9. Answers
will vary. 10. Answers will vary.

Page 60
Answers will vary.

Page 61
Answers will vary.

Page 62
Answers will vary.

Page 63
1. saw; 2. fall; 3. star; 4. roll; 5. back

Page 64–75
Answers will vary.

Page 76
Uppercase and lowercase letters
should be in appropriate tables.

1. are; 2. wants; 3. writes; 4. eat;
5. is

Page 77
Nouns

Person: dad, mother

Place: bedroom, school

Thing: chair, swing

Idea: love, freedom

Proper Nouns

Person: Mrs. Wu, Casey

Place: America, Florida

Thing: Friday, January

Page 78
1. furry; 2. loud; 3. round;
4. bumpy; 5. tough; 6. sandy;
7. soft; 8. sweet

Page 79
1. or; 2. but; 3. and; 4. but; 5. or;
6. but; 7. and; 8. and

Page 80
1. an; 2. a; 3. a; 4. a; 5. an; 6. a;
7. an; 8. a; 9. a; 10. a

Page 81
1. in; 2. on; 3. at; 4. behind;
5. around; 6. across; 7. over;
8. inside; 9. down

Page 82
1. A; 2. E; 3. A; 4. T; 5. E; 6. C; 7. T;
8. A; 9. T; 10. C

Page 83
1. Elias was going to the store.
2. Henry felt very happy.
3. Would you take me to the
lake? 4. Can you see the big
jet? 5. Mother told me to eat my
dinner. 6. We; 7. She; 8. He; 9. It;
10. They

Page 84
1. eggs, flour, and butter; 2. salad,
pears, and bread; 3. Joannie,
Grace, and Sam; 4. yellow, black,
and gray; 5. turkey, tomato, and
lettuce; 6. games, puzzles, and
cards; 7. lions, elephants, and
tigers; 8. balloons, cake, and
streamers; 9. February 4, 2010;
10. November 12, 2014

Page 85
1. Preview: to look before, or
Review: to look again; 2. Untie:
to take ties apart; 3. Retake: to
take again; 4. Restless: to be
without rest, or Restful: to be full
of rest; 5. Helpful: to be full of
help, or Helpless: without help; 6.
Buildable: able to be built

Page 86
Fruits We Eat: apple, banana,
orange, pear

Things We Wear: coat, glove, hat,
scarf

Things We Eat With: bowl, dish,
fork, spoon

Answer Key

Page 87

Birds that Swim: duck, goose, penguin, swan

Large Cats: bobcat, jaguar, lion, tiger

Green Reptiles: iguana, lizard, snake, turtle

Page 88

Green Vegetables: broccoli, cucumber, lettuce, peas

Things with Wheels: bike, car, skateboard, tricycle

Ice-Cream Flavors: chocolate, mint, strawberry, vanilla

Page 90

Answers will vary.

Notes

Notes

Carson-Dellosa Publishing

Common Core ALIGNED State Standards

Common Core Connections: Language Arts is the perfect tool for helping students master Common Core language arts skills. The easy-to-use format provides a skill assessment to determine learning gaps and then offers individualized remediation. The skill assessment analysis correlates to focused practice pages. The practice pages are perfect for targeting and strengthening specific Common Core standards for individual students. A standards correlation is printed on each practice page and is also found in the comprehensive matrix, allowing for easy and efficient planning and documentation. Each page includes "I Can" statements to encourage self-assessment and reflection!

Check out these other great Carson-Dellosa products to support Common Core instruction in your classroom.

CenterSOLUTIONS® for the Common Core Task Cards CD-140333

CenterSOLUTIONS® for the Common Core Thinking Mats CD-140339

Common Core Language Arts 4 Today: Daily Skill Practice CD-104596

Common Core Connections: Math CD-104602

Common Core State Standards Kit CD-158169

ISBN 978-1-62442-793-0

Carson-Dellosa Publishing, LLC
PO Box 35665
Greensboro, NC 27425 USA

Visit
learningspotlibrary.com
for FREE activities!

Printed in the USA

0 44222 23225 2

carsondellosa.com